THIS BOOK BELONGS TO

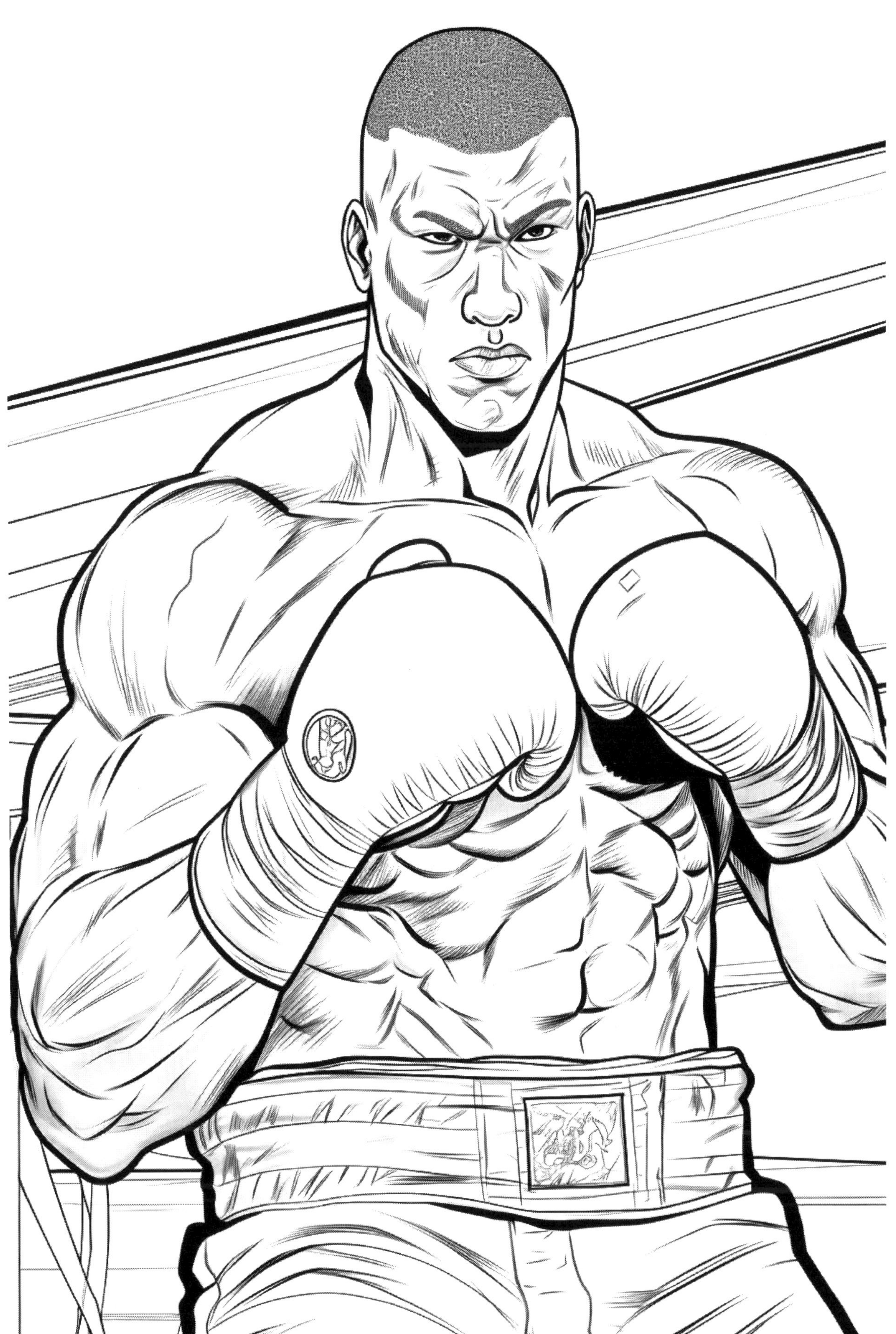

97

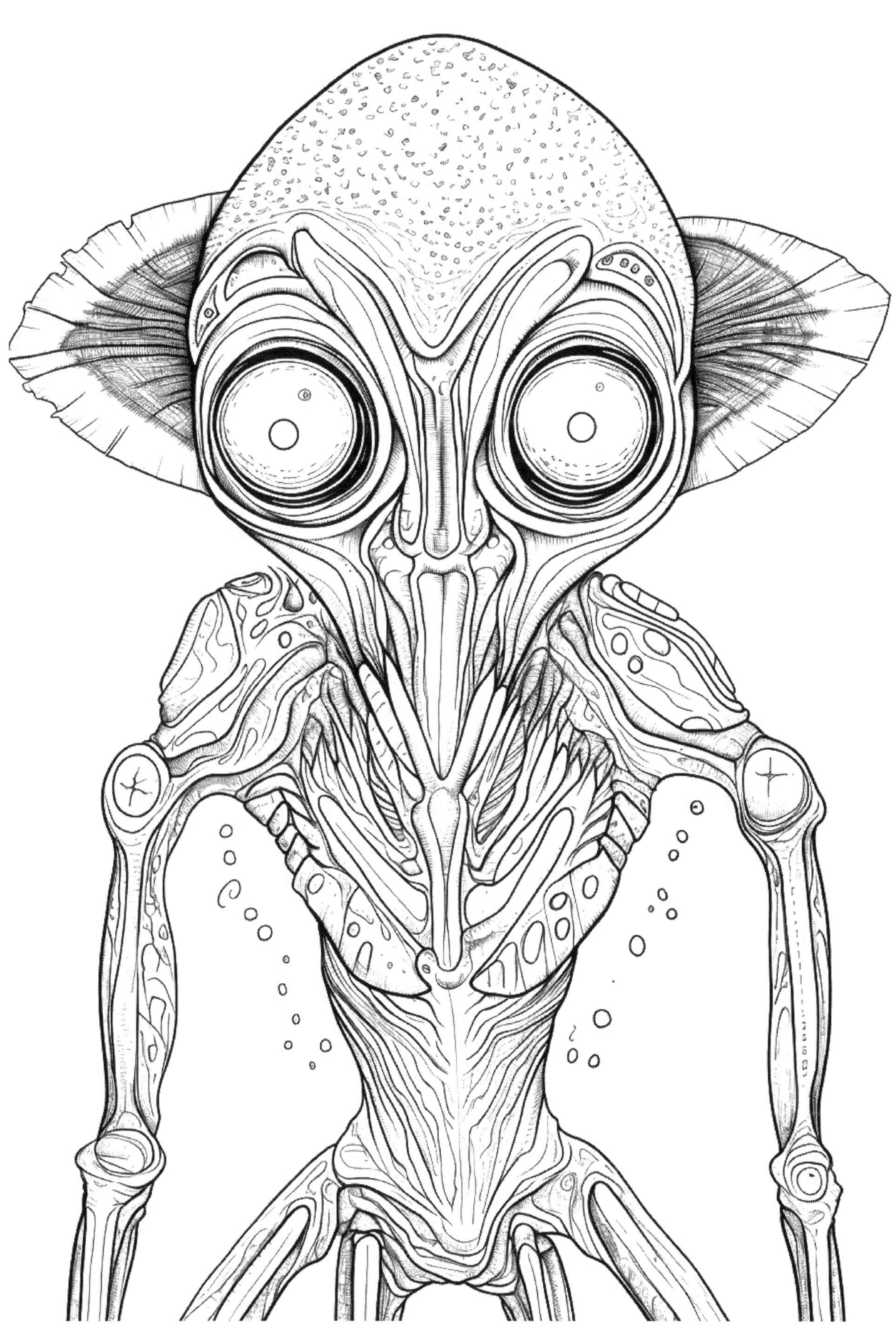

We want to extend a heartfelt thank you for choosing our coloring book!

If you loved our book and appreciated our coloring pages, we kindly ask that you consider leaving us a positive review.

Your opinion means the world to us and will help us improve our work and reach more people who share your interests.

Thank you again for your support, and happy coloring!

Made in the USA
Columbia, SC
16 May 2023